TRACING LETTERS

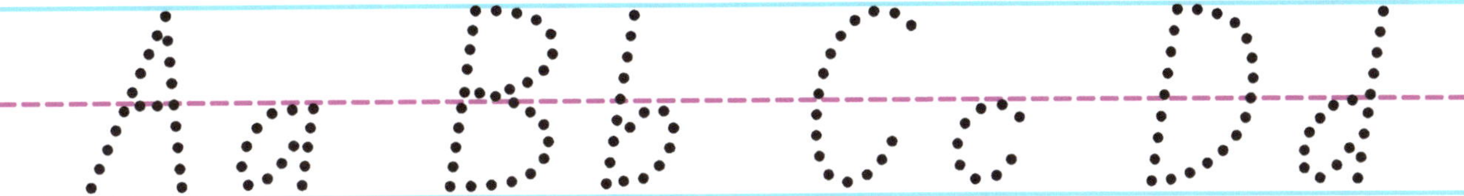

ant
Aa

A A A A A

A

G G G G G G

G

bee
Bb

B B B B B

B

b b b b b b

b

Bee / bee

camel
Cc

C C C C C

C

C C C C C

C

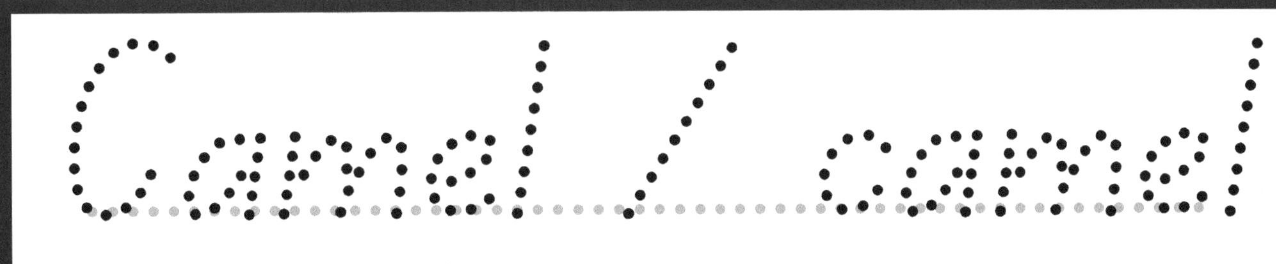

Camel / camel

dinosaur
Dd

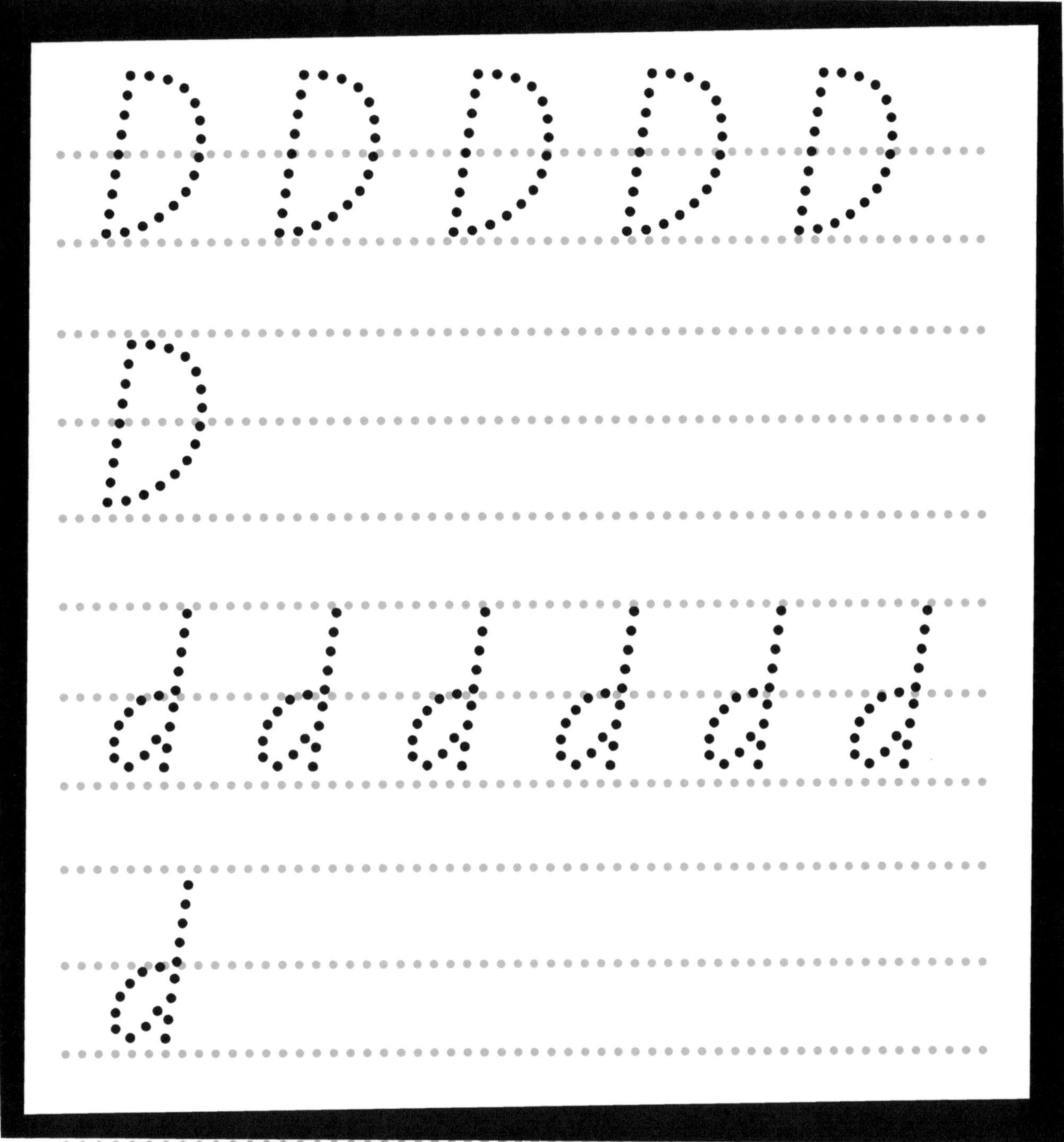

Dinosaur / dinosaur

Ee
elephant

fish
Ff

FFFFF

F

fffff

f

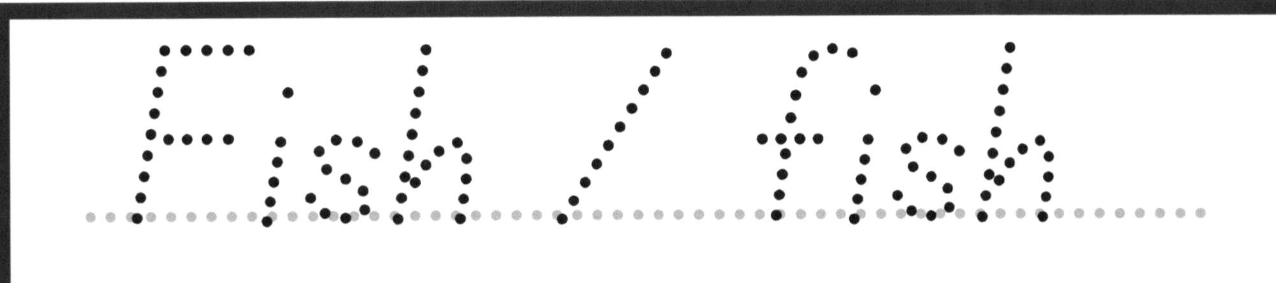

grasshopper
Gg

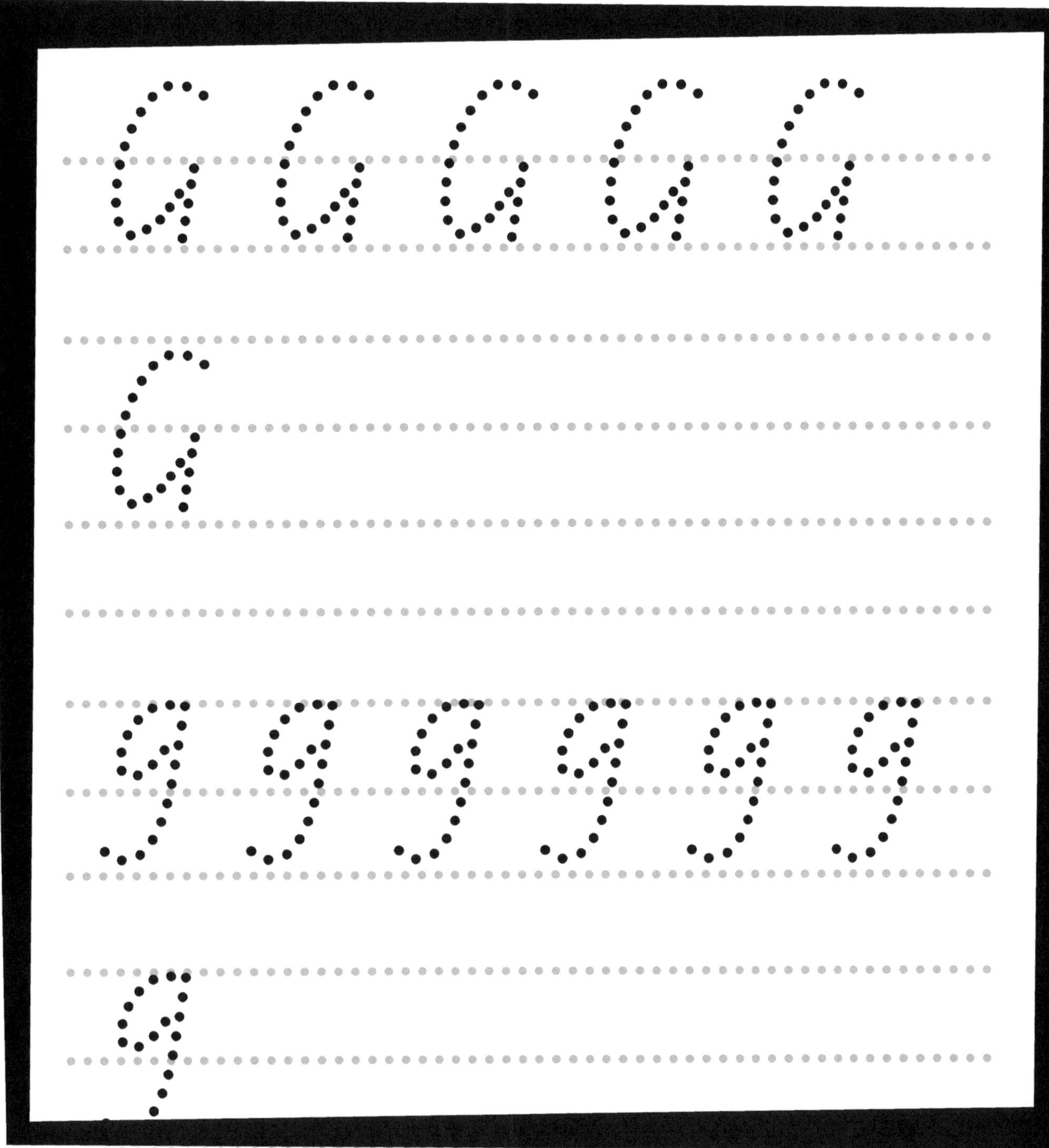

Grasshopper / grasshopper

hippo
Hh

H H H H H H H

H

h h h h h h h

h

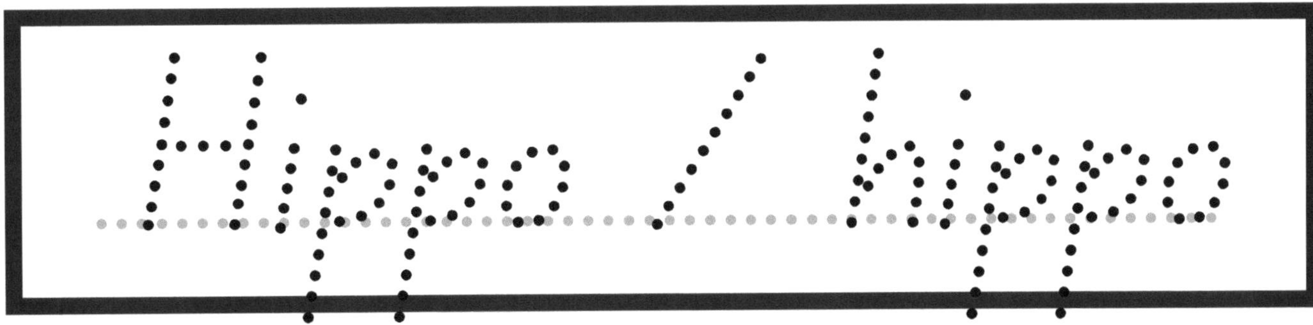

iguana
I i

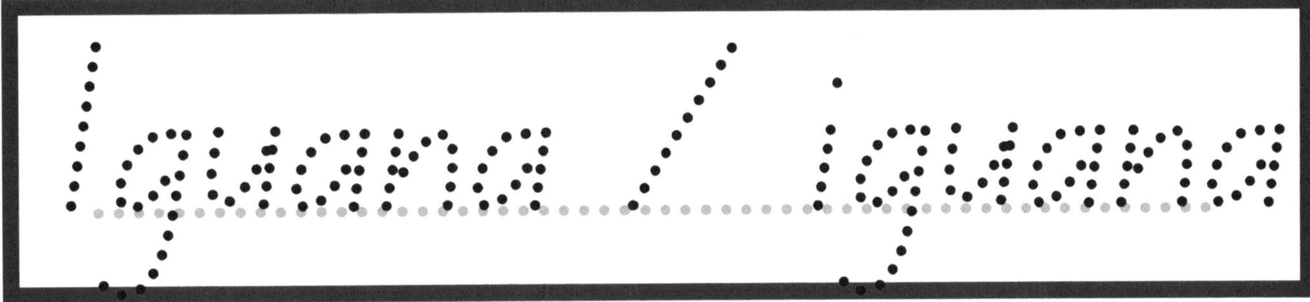

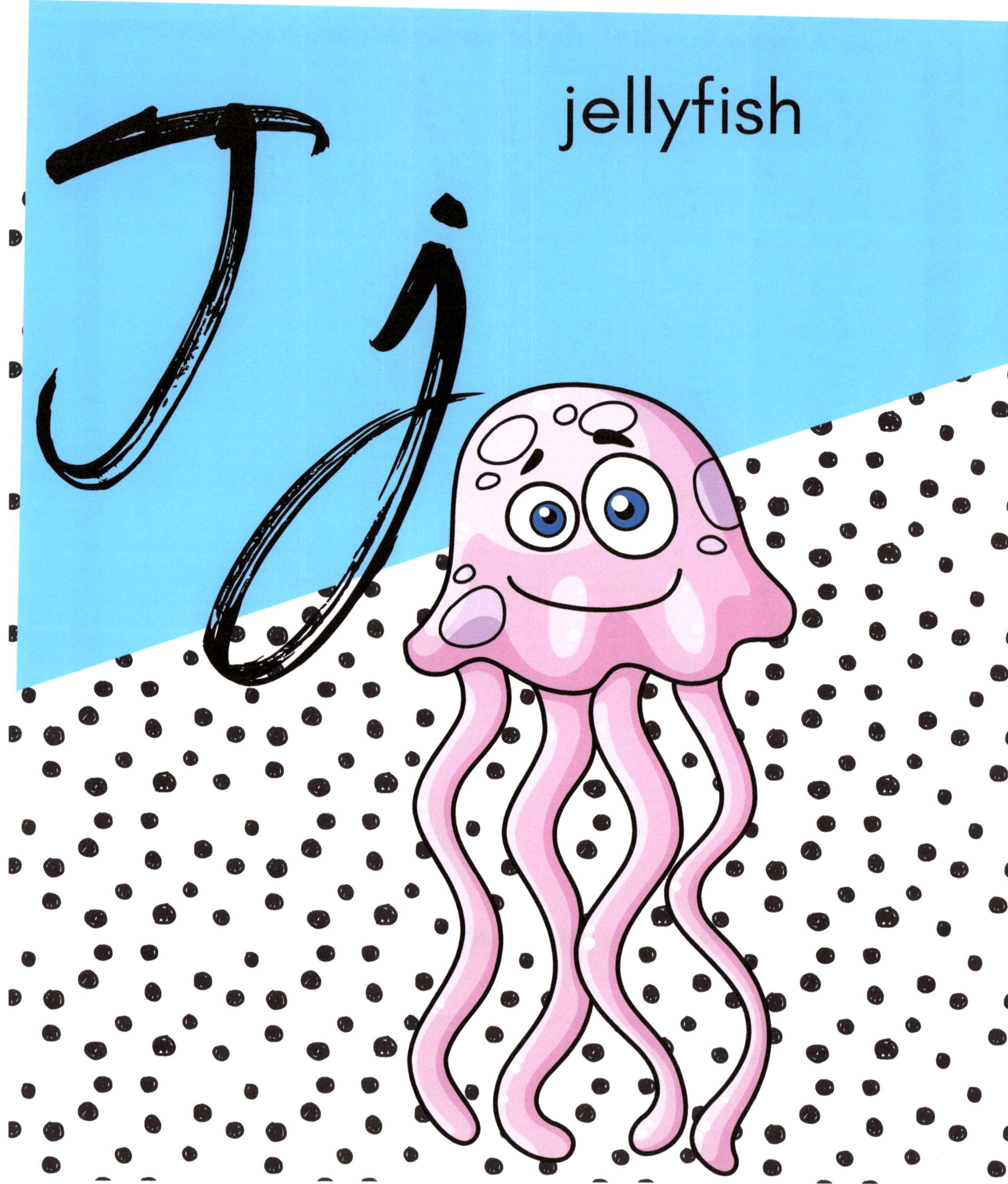

jellyfish

J J J J J

J

JJJJJ

j

Kk
kangaroo

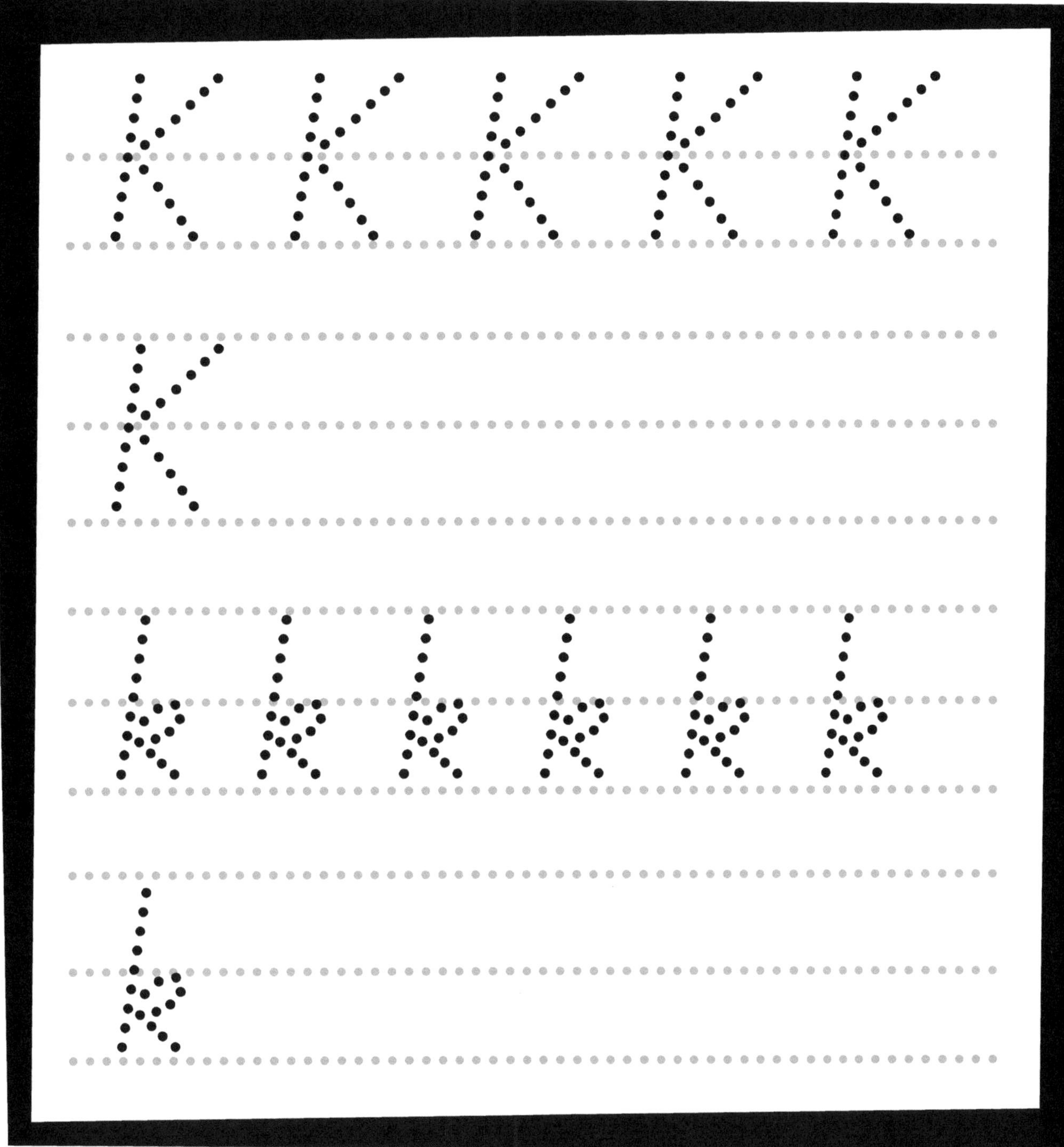

lion

L L L L L

L

l l l l l l l l

l

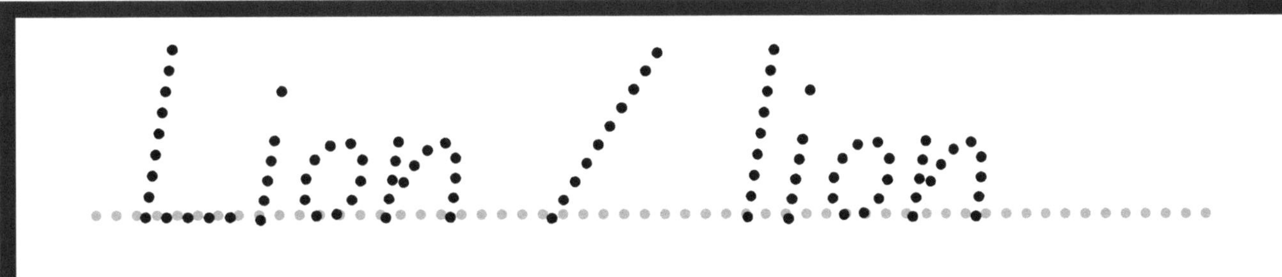

monkey
Mm

M M M M M M M M

M

m m m m m

m

Nn
narwhal

N N N N N N

N

n n n n n n

n

octopus
Oo

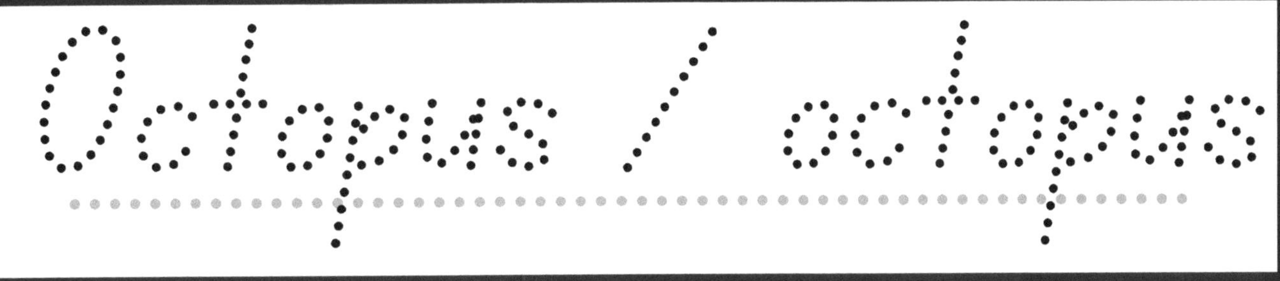

Octopus / octopus

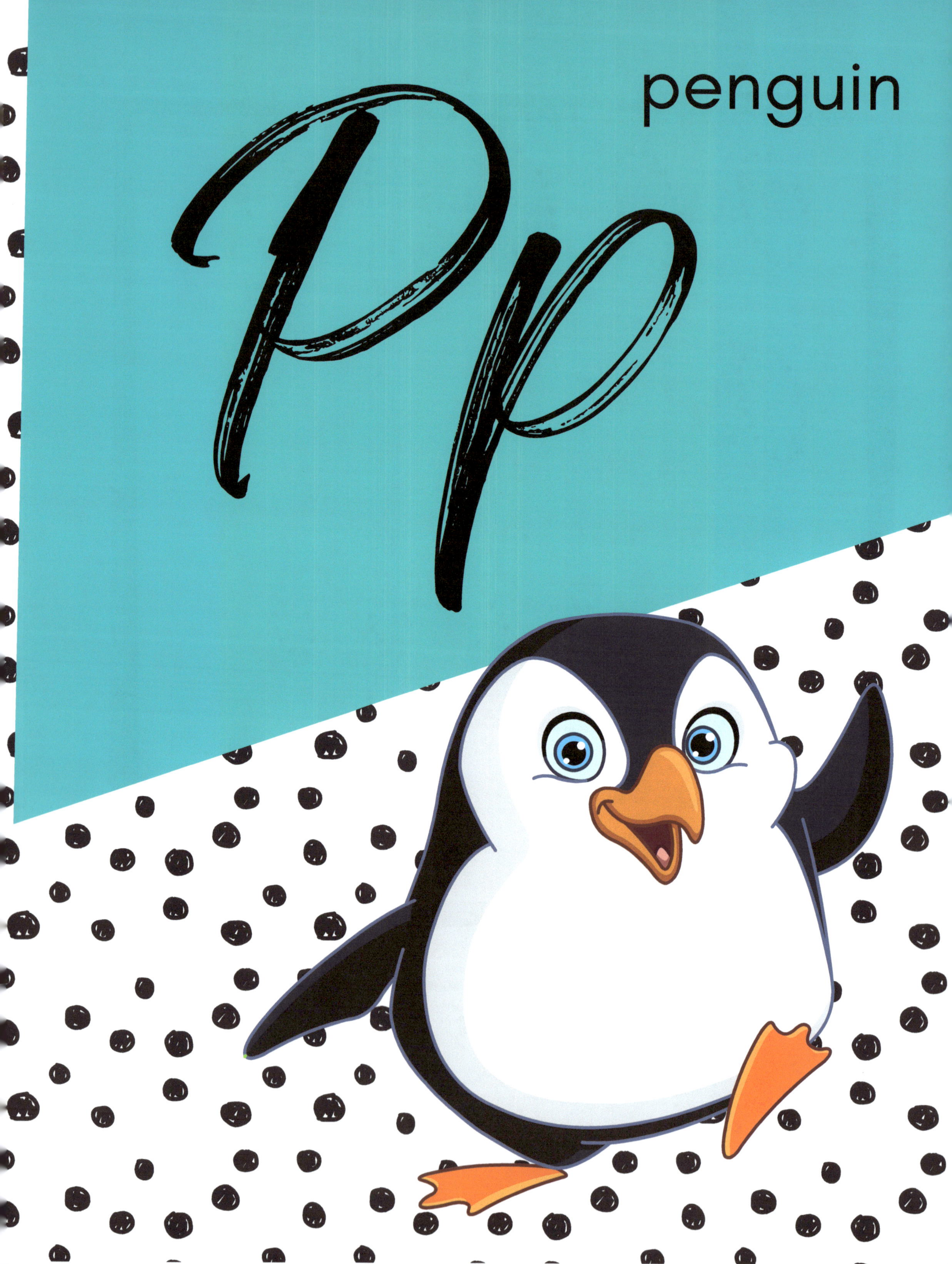
penguin
Pp

P P P P P

P

P P P P P

P

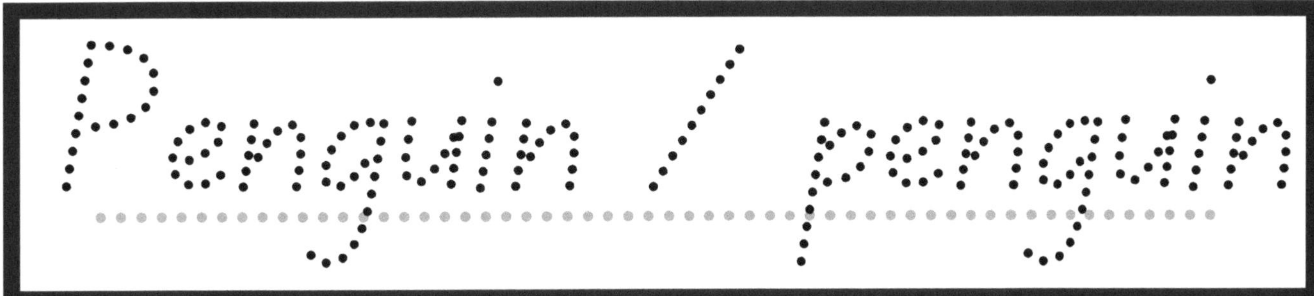

queen bee
Qq

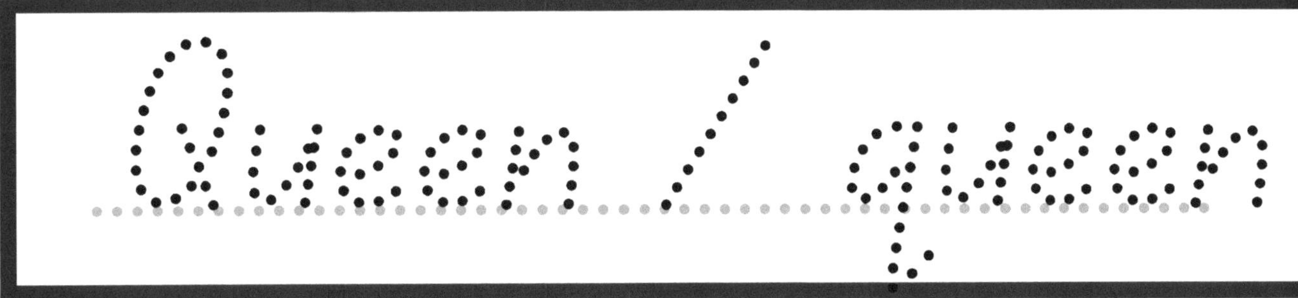

Rr
rabbit

R R R R R

R

r r r r r

r

snake
Ss

S S S S S

S

S S S S S S

S

Tt
tiger

TTTTT
T
ttttt
t

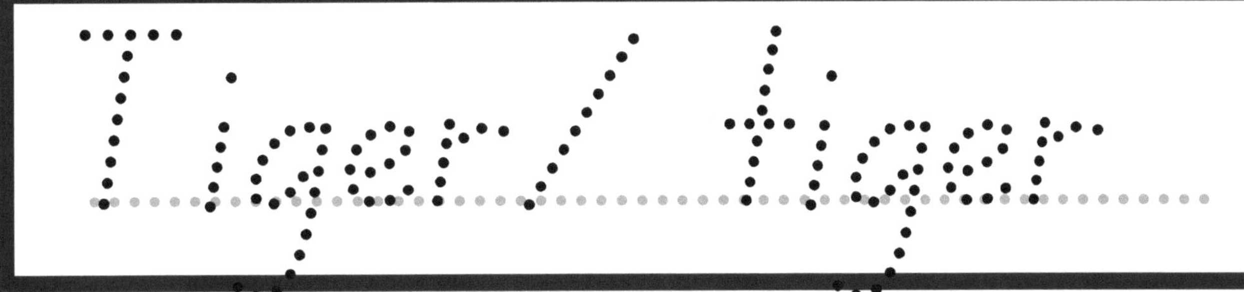

Uu
unicorn

Unicorn / unicorn

W
vulture

Y Y Y Y Y Y

Y

v v v v v v

v

Vulture / vulture

whale
Ww

Whale / whale

x-ray fish
Xx

X x

X X X X X

X

x x x x x x

x

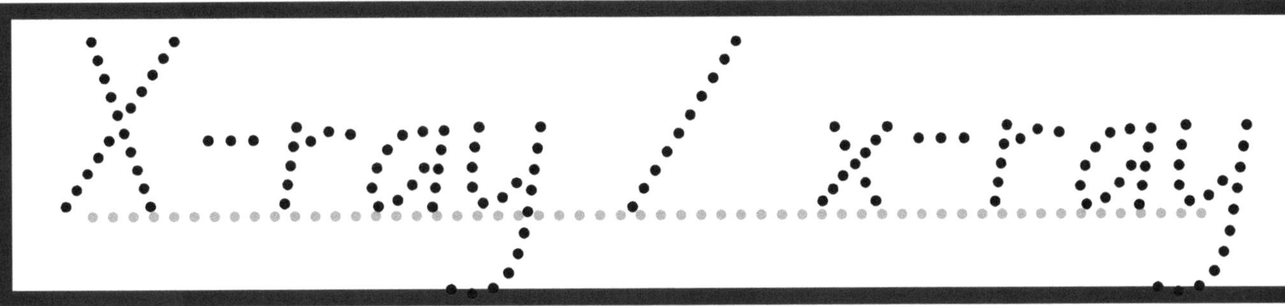

yak
Yy

Y Y Y Y Y Y Y

Y

y y y y y y

y

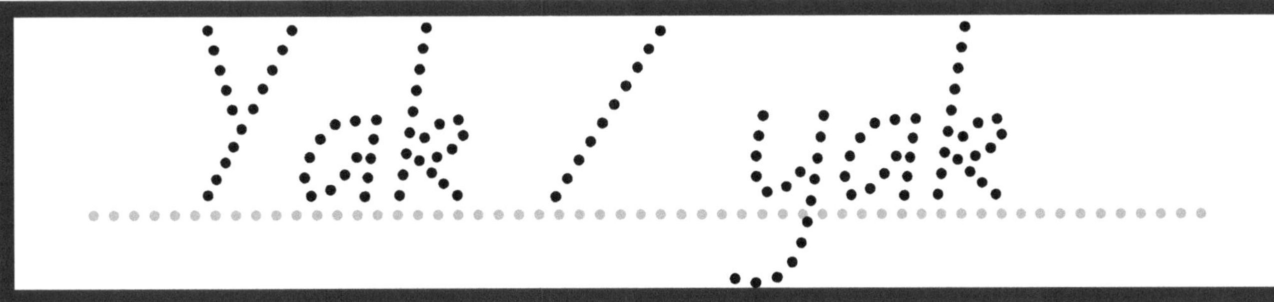

Zz
zebra

Numbers

MARK ONE CIRCLE

1
one

one one one one

DRAW ONE STAR

MARK TWO CIRCLES

○ ○ ○ ○

○ ○ ○ ○

○ ○ ○ ○

○ ○ ○ ○

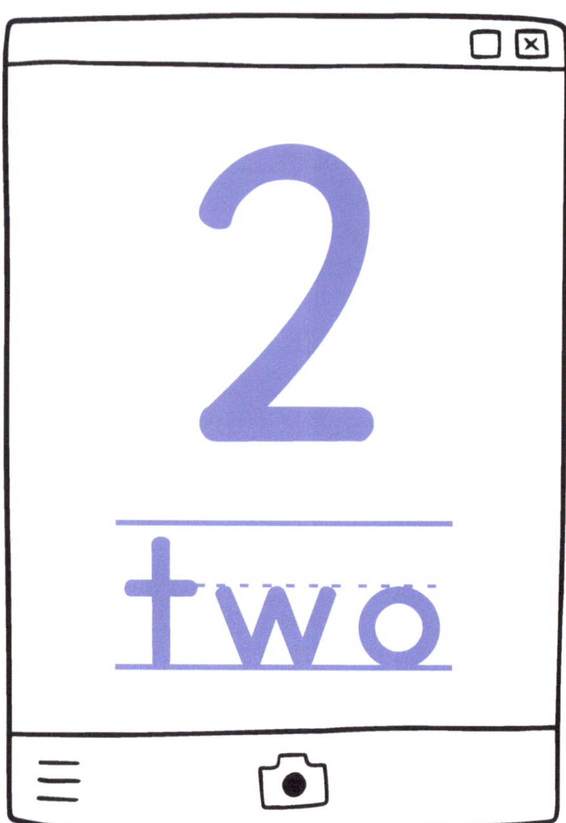

2 2 2 2 2 2

two two two

O O O O

O O O O

O O O O

O O O O

3 3 3 3 3 3

three three

MARK FOUR CIRCLES

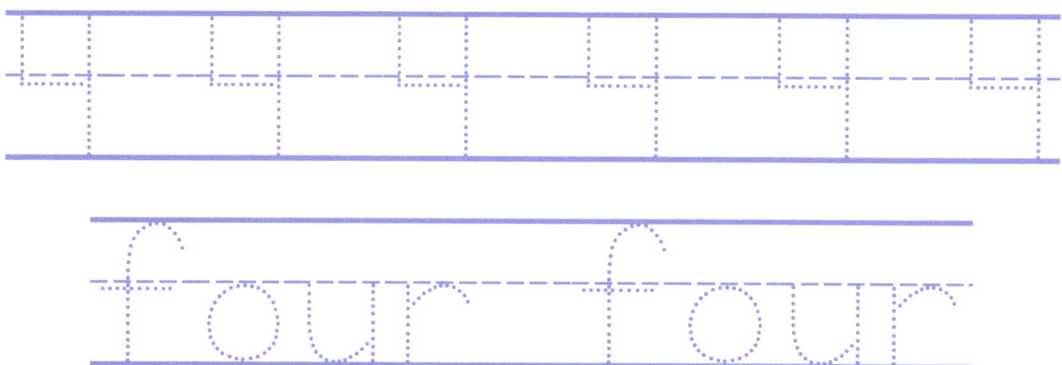

MARK FIVE CIRCLES

MARK SIX CIRCLES

Name: ______________________   Date: ______________________

O   O   O   O

O   O   O   O

O   O   O   O

O   O   O   O

MARK EIGHT CIRCLES

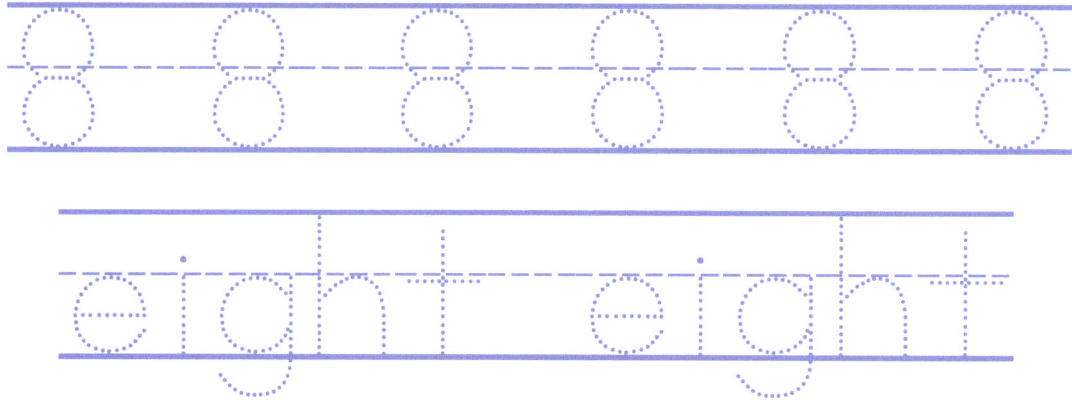

MARK NINE CIRCLES

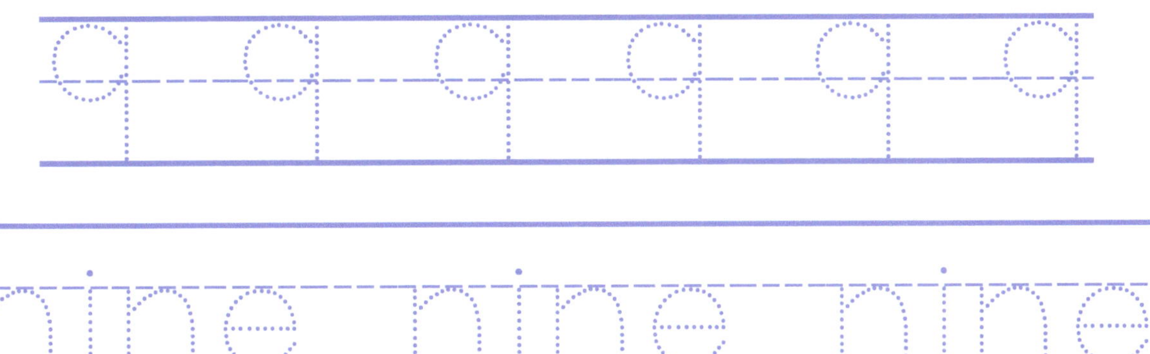

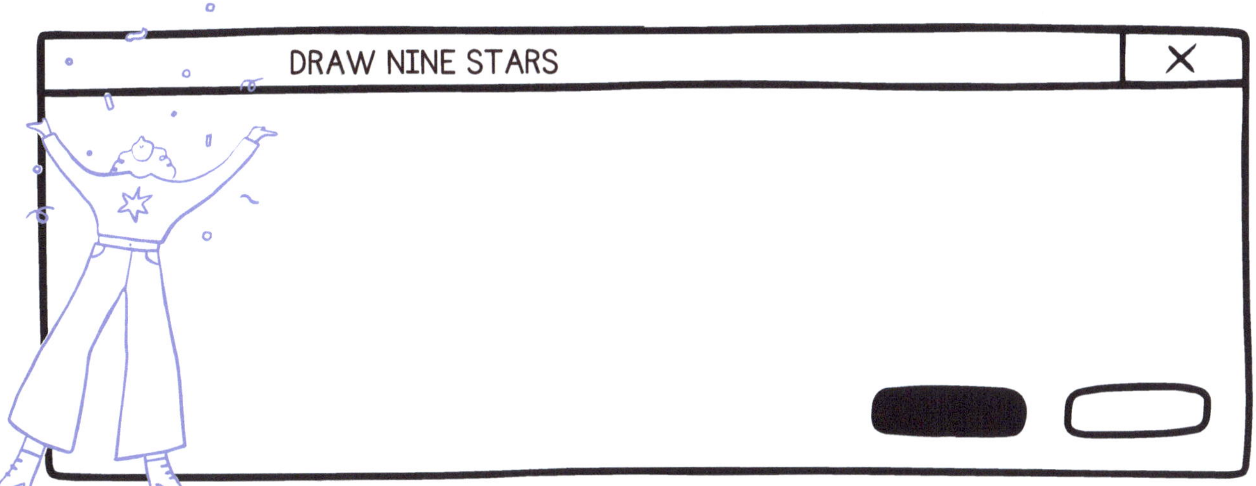

MARK TEN CIRCLES

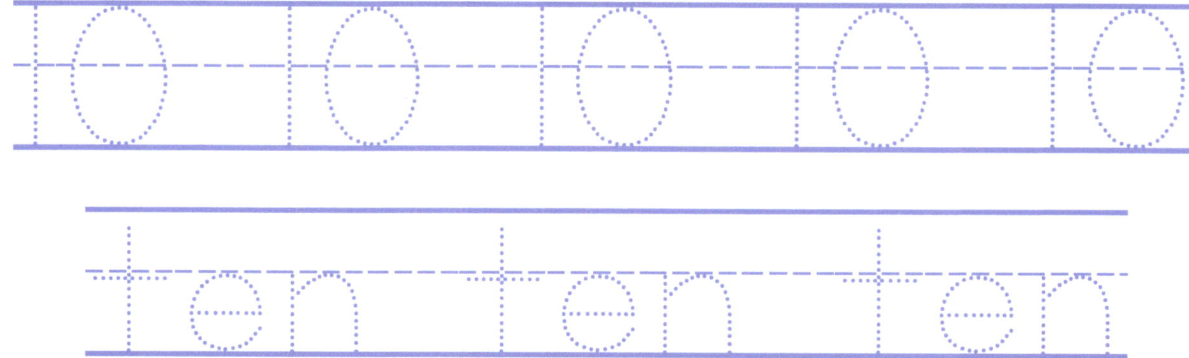